SNOWY OWL

SNOWY OWL

A Visual Natural History   PAUL BANNICK

MOUNTAINEERS
BOOKS

For Tom Campion, a relentless champion of Arctic lands & wildlife

 MOUNTAINEERS BOOKS is dedicated
to the exploration, preservation, and enjoyment
of outdoor and wilderness areas.

1001 SW Klickitat Way, Suite 201, Seattle, WA 98134
800-553-4453, www.mountaineersbooks.org

Printed in China
Distributed in the United Kingdom by Cordee, www.cordee.co.uk

23 22 21 20   1 2 3 4 5

Copyeditor: Linda Gunnarson
Design and layout: Kate Basart/Union Pageworks
All photographs by the author unless credited otherwise

Front cover, jacket: *A Snowy Owl flies aggressively toward a rival in an effort to dislodge it from a favored driftwood perch.* Back cover, jacket: *Strong headwinds do not deter Snowy Owls, whose compact bodies and strong wings are built for hunting in extreme Arctic environments.* Front jacket flap: *Six nestling Snowy Owls press against one another for warmth as they await the return of their mother to their nest on the Arctic tundra.* Front cover, case: *A Snowy Owl turns to follow the course of a lemming scampering across the tundra below.* Back cover, case: *A female Snowy Owl and her young atop a natural mound on the Arctic tundra await a prey delivery from the male.* Frontispiece: *A Snowy Owl begins hunting at sunset amid the blowing snow. Snowy Owls are often active at times when other owls would remain on roosts.* Opposite: *Snowy Owls thrive where the white of snow, the gold of the tundra, and the blue of the sea trade dominance over the seasons of the year. Here, a Snowy takes flight with the rising sun.* Page 128: *A nearly pure white male Snowy Owl hunts from a snow-covered tundra mound. Snowy Owls with this coloring are usually older males and are extremely difficult to see when perched on snow.*

Library of Congress Cataloging-in-Publication data is on file for this title at https://lccn.loc.gov/2020004718

Mountaineers Books titles may be purchased for corporate, educational, or other promotional sales, and our authors
are available for a wide range of events. For information on special discounts or booking an author, contact our
customer service at 800-553-4453 or mbooks@mountaineersbooks.org.

Printed on FSC®-certified materials

ISBN: 978-1-68051-315-8

An independent nonprofit publisher since 1960

Preface

A wintering Snowy Owl perched atop a telephone pole at my boyhood home near Seattle was the first owl, of any kind, that I had ever seen. I would not see another Snowy until more than thirty years later, when I finally found and photographed one in British Columbia.

Since then, I have spent tens of thousands of hours in the field in an effort to better understand these owls. I have observed and photographed Snowy Owls during all twelve months and all four seasons, including more than a dozen trips to the Arctic. I photographed at tundra nests over three seasons, often staying in a blind for days at a time with little, if any, sleep, enveloped in dense clouds of mosquitoes and hoping not to be visited by a polar bear. I successfully watched courtship during two seasons yet failed to even find owls on several other trips. I photographed the owls dispersing out of the Arctic in the fall and wintering on the Great Plains as well as in Washington, Oregon, Minnesota, British Columbia, Alberta, and Manitoba. Spring and fall temperatures in the Arctic and winter temperatures elsewhere often hovered between negative 10 and negative 40 degrees Fahrenheit, with winds frequently ripping at my face. The warmest gloves did not allow me the dexterity needed to operate my camera; my eyes froze shut at the lashes; face coverings directed my breath to my glasses, viewfinder, and camera LCD, coating each with ice and forcing me to scrape view holes in order to resume my photography. Batteries died after a few hours, and cameras froze. There were many disappointing days when snowstorms, windstorms, thick fog, or absent owls forced me to change my plans or when I remained stormbound at an airport for days.

Each challenge, discomfort, or inconvenience was absolutely worth it, as I was able to observe and capture intimate moments rarely if ever preserved with a camera. Decades of research and field time allowed me to better understand what I was

A Snowy Owl hunts from the top of a tombstone on a snowy fall morning. Snowy Owls prefer to hunt from elevated perches, often in short supply on the flat tundra.

observing and when it was new or significant. Each experience, whether a failure or a success, taught me more about the life of the Snowy Owl.

   With this book, I've worked to bring the life of the Snowy Owl into greater focus for everyone. As researchers gain more clarity in understanding each stage of the complex life of the Snowy Owl, I hope that my photographs and field experiences add further context, helping us to learn more about the owl and to make choices that can help ensure its long-term survival with us on this planet.

—Paul Bannick
Seattle, Washington

Snowy Owls can be active at any hour, but are most active after sunset, before sunrise, or when the sun is obscured by clouds.

TUNDRA MYSTERY

The powerful voice felt like it emanated from the very soul of the tundra—the ethereal hoots of a male owl pulsing forcefully in the distance. Waves of ice fog swirled around me, and I knew it was risky to stand there alone, up to my knees in snow, on the Arctic tundra at one o'clock on an April morning. But I was hoping against odds to witness and photograph Snowy Owl courtship, a process so rarely captured on film or video that all of the books and academic resources that I had been able to find relied upon illustrations. This courtship ritual, like so much of the behavior and history of this owl, had been shrouded in mystery. Being cold and alone in the fog suddenly seemed appropriate for my situation.

The Snowy Owl's hoarse but resonant *hoo hoo hoo hoo* has been reported to carry for up to two miles, so I had no idea how far away the owl I heard might be. But my skin tingled at the thought of having finally found an "advertising" Snowy Owl after years of trying. I trudged forward through the snow and fog, at times unable to see more than a stride ahead, carefully dropping each snowshoe, choosing drifts of soft snow instead of the crusty ice of frozen tundra or the slick ice overlaying a pond or lake. I didn't want to break through the ice to deep water, slip, or make too much noise, which might frighten a vigilant owl.

Occasional gusts of arctic wind briefly opened vignettes of clarity in an otherwise opaque landscape. A white shape lunging forward through the bank of fog revealed itself as a calling male Snowy Owl atop a tundra mound, lemming in bill, entreating a female to consider his gift of food. Another breeze closed that view, but an hour or so later, shifting winds unveiled the owl bouncing through the air just above the horizon. Exaggerated and slow, downward wingbeats pushed his white feathery body steeply up and above the ceiling of fog; then as his stiff wings raised vertically, he dropped groundward and back into the fog. Again, he flew up

TOP: *A male Snowy Owl performs an undulating flight display to potential mates, calling while airborne and holding a lemming in his bill. Exaggerated downward wing strokes lift the male up, followed by long pauses with his wings in a stiff, vertical position and tail spread, which allow him to glide down.*

BOTTOM: *This bouncy flight ends when the male lowers his head and floats down to the tundra to begin his ground display.*

on the strong downstrokes, resulting in a moth-like dance against the wind and in and out of the fog and my sight.

These gripping moments punctuated my attempts over many weeks to track, observe, and photograph Snowy Owl courtship. Each opportunity ended up swallowed in the fog, followed by hours or sometimes days without sight or sound. Gradually I learned where and when to look and at last was rewarded when the owl drifted down from the clouds, talons falling into view first, then his torso, head, and finally the raised wings, landing softly with his back to me atop a tundra mound. Slowly he lowered his wingtips but held his shoulders stiff and high, like a conductor about to begin a symphony, before he spread his wings and tail and started calling. The call sounded more intense as he turned toward me, revealing an enormous lemming in his bill. He held this posture as he turned in a circle, lifting his feet and stamping into the soft snow, his raised wings fixed. His eyes squinted as he forced his calls aggressively across the tundra, then opened at each pause. Although I was more than a hundred yards away, I didn't dare risk disturbing this rare moment by trying to get closer. I watched as the male displayed in this manner at several different mounds without response.

Then one morning around four o'clock, as I paused along a ridgeline, I sensed movement. I turned my head in time to watch a bulky white shape flying quickly just above the ice toward a raised mound. I could barely make out the ivory male displaying against the equally white snow when a female landed behind him. The rhythm of his display did not change; with spread wings and tail he continued calling and turning. Initially the female showed a surprising indifference to the male's display, shifting her gaze between watching him and scanning the horizon, until eventually her eyes seemed transfixed upon his wings. Holding a lemming in his bill, he waved it side to side, occasionally teasing her with a glimpse of the potential reward, only to continue hiding it as he danced and she watched. Then the fog enveloped the mound and the owls for the remainder of the morning.

I cannot be certain what happened next. I like to think the female was compelled by the male to mate and that the two chose that tundra mound as their nest

Male Snowy Owls initiate the ground component of their courtship display by lifting their wings at the shoulders and turning in circles atop a prominent mound. Oftentimes they will hold a lemming in their bill and call during such displays.

Snowy Owls are mostly nocturnal during the winter when they frequently hunt unsuspecting waterbirds along shorelines.

and raised a large brood, progeny that one day will migrate south to a place where a large number of people might see them and be entranced by their mystery and moved by their beauty to learn more about Snowy Owls and their lives.

The Snowy Owl—also known as the Snow Owl, Snowy White Owl, Arctic Owl, and White Owl—is one of the most easily identified but least understood owls in the world. Most of its life is shrouded from our view. We know that the owls hatch from eggs on the Arctic tundra, often hundreds of miles from the nearest human. Fledgling birds disperse in all directions and in most cases live out nomadic lives on remote, windswept, treeless expanses in some of the least populated areas of the Northern Hemisphere.

Because Snowy Owls are often hidden from us by inaccessibility, extreme weather, or darkness, our impressions of them have largely been shaped by owl mythology. We have long been fascinated with them: the Snowy Owl is believed to be one of the oldest bird species depicted in prehistoric cave art with an image found at Les Trois Frères, estimated to be 17,000 years old. Popular myths related to Snowy Owl behaviors, anthropomorphized portrayals such as Harry Potter's pet owl, Hedwig, and the occasional inaccurate media story perpetuate misunderstandings. Without firsthand experience it is easy to make broad assumptions about their behaviors, their populations, and their future.

In recent years, however, dedicated researchers have helped us better understand this mysterious Arctic icon. We have learned more about the behaviors of the "Snowy," as many affectionately refer to this owl, and also that it is a critical indicator species. The presence and health of Snowy Owl populations reflect the larger conditions and health of the Arctic's tundra habitat and its other resident species, including polar bears, musk oxen, Arctic foxes, eiders, loons, and dozens of other birds that live, hunt, migrate through, or nest on the tundra.

A group of musk oxen graze upon grasses, willows, lichen, roots, and mosses on the Arctic tundra. Musk oxen move into the mountains during the winter when the snow becomes too deep at lower elevations.

An Arctic fox prances across the tundra. These canines turn white in winter to camouflage against the snow and change to brown or gray in the spring to blend into the summer tundra.

A Snowy Owl attacks an Arctic fox. They pursue the same prey and sometimes the foxes try to take Snowy Owl eggs or flightless young owls.

ABOVE: *A male Willow Ptarmigan, in his early spring courtship plumage of brown and white, prances with his red eye-comb raised in an effort to impress a potential mate.*

OPPOSITE: *Conflict frequently erupts between competitors for lemmings. Here, a Short-eared Owl shadows a Rough-legged Hawk in an effort to drive it from the area.*

A Red-throated Loon prepares to take flight from an Arctic tundra pond, just yards from a Snowy Owl nest. The Red-throated Loon breeds in arctic and subarctic regions of Eurasia and North America.

Snowy Owls nest on Arctic tundra mounds that are often near tundra ponds, streams, or the ocean.

Among the first migratory birds to arrive on their breeding grounds on the Arctic tundra, a migrating flock of King Eiders flies over the territory of courting Snowy Owls. Because they congregate in large flocks, far from shore and in ice-prone areas, King Eider populations could be hit hard by an offshore oil spill in Arctic waters.

PHYSICAL FEATURES

The Snowy Owl (*Bubo scandiacus*) is by far the easiest owl to identify and is unlikely to be confused with any other. So distinctive is the Snowy that it was put in its own genus, *Nyctea*, in 1809 before it was reclassified in 2003 as a member of the *Bubo* genus, which includes the Great Horned Owl and Eagle Owl.

The Great Horned Owl is the Snowy Owl's closest living relative, but only the lightest-colored Great Horned Owls of the paler Arctic race approach the color of the darkest female Snowy Owl. Snowys are also more compact and have rounder heads than Great Horned Owls. Snowy Owls often share habitat with Short-eared Owls, but the latter has a more distinctive facial disk, is browner, and has a striped rather than a white breast. I also know of several occasions when people mistook pale Barn Owls in their headlights for Snowy Owls due to their light color—and perhaps a bit of wishful thinking. The Snowy Owl is much larger and bulkier than the Barn Owl and lacks its heart-shaped facial disk.

The Snowy Owl is one of the largest owls in the world, with females weighing up to 6.5 pounds and having a wingspan of up to 61 inches. The females are roughly 25 percent heavier than the males, which max out at 4.5 pounds, with a wingspan of up to 56 inches. The two genders have a similar body length of about 23.5 inches. The Snowy is the largest owl in North America in terms of weight, but has a shorter body length than the lighter Great Gray Owl and a wingspan similar to both the Great Gray Owl and the Great Horned Owl.

Although they are often referred to as "earless," Snowy Owls have small ear tufts that are rarely seen except when they are flying against a strong wind or when females are on the nest. An owl's ear tufts have nothing to do with hearing, but rather are believed to help hide the owl by breaking up its shape. The Snowy Owl's tufts might play that role, they might signal an owl's mood, or they may simply be

Snowy Owls display several adaptations to the Arctic environment including thick feathers around the bill and on the feet to keep the owl warm as well as a heavy, compact build and strong wings that help them fly into strong winds.

LEFT: *A Snowy Owl takes flight from a tombstone in a graveyard on the Arctic tundra.*

OPPOSITE: *The dark markings on the Snowy Owl's white feathers help hide it on the windswept Arctic tundra, where dark vegetation often pushes through the snow from the fall through the spring, and patches of white snow may linger into the summer.*

ABOVE: *A female Snowy Owl, with ear-tufts raised and eyes open, reacts to the fast approach of a Pomarine Jaeger. Some speculate that these tufts may signal the mood of an owl.*

OPPOSITE: *Many Snowy Owls spend much of their lives near water. Here, a Snowy Owl takes flight from the sand of a Pacific coast beach.*

vestiges from an "eared" ancestor. For hearing, an owl's facial disk funnels sound to openings (ears) hidden by feathers on both sides of its skull.

Since worldwide Snowy Owl populations regularly mix, there is no geographic variation in the color or pattern of Snowy Owls across the globe, but they do have sex-specific feather patterns, a feature rare among owls.

The legs of this large-bodied white owl are so heavily feathered that feathers even cover the toes. The large eyes are yellow or orange-yellow on a face with a less distinctive facial disk than that of most other owls. The long, dense rictal bristles that nearly hide the black bill may help warm the air the owl breathes during particularly cold weather, or they may be used as a sensory tool for an otherwise near-sighted owl, or perhaps for something else entirely. Although Snowy Owls do not see well close up, they are believed to have the best distance vision of any owl.

These are among the many physical adaptations Snowy Owls have made to their Arctic homes. In fact, they are one of a handful of birds, including Gyrfalcons, ravens, Willow Ptarmigan, redpolls, gulls, murres, and guillemots, that can be found year-round on or near the Arctic tundra, surviving temperatures of negative 40 degrees Fahrenheit and even lower. One study concluded that the Snowy Owl's thermal conductance is second among birds only to the Adélie Penguin and is also roughly equal to that of the Arctic fox and Dall sheep.

It is not known precisely how long Snowy Owls live, but individual birds have lived twenty years in the wild and thirty years in captivity. We do know that young owls are the most vulnerable, but once owls mature, they survive at a much higher rate.

Vocalizations

Like other owls, Snowy Owls have a broad vocal repertoire, but they are far less vocal than most outside the breeding season. During the winter, I hear them only when one owl is flying close to or landing near another owl. Sometimes during those encounters, both birds hiss with their bills open. In contrast, during courtship and breeding they emit a wide range of hoots, grunts, chitters, and screams

Snowy Owls emit some of the sounds in their vocal repertoire without opening their bills.

that are often associated with gender. Female calls are generally higher pitched. Vocalization during autumn's dispersal falls somewhere in between, with newly independent juvenile owls regularly scolding other young Snowy Owls, Arctic foxes, dogs, and even people with their open-mouthed screeches as they bob their heads up and down and from side to side.

Territorial, or advertising, hooting is how the male communicates the area he will defend and how he attracts a mate. The female hoots much more rarely. The first time I witnessed a hooting Snowy Owl I was struck by the power of his voice, but also by how much his calling posture resembled that of the Great Horned Owl.

Like the Great Horned, the Snowy fills his throat with air and with each hoot bows his head, lowers his wings, lifts his tail, and lunges forward roughly parallel to the ground. Often, he closes his eyes (or nearly does) when his hooting is most intense. To me, the Snowy Owl's call sounds coarser than the Great Horned Owl's, like a foghorn, and with much less tonal variation.

Sex-Distinguishing Characteristics

Snowy Owls are among the few owls for which older adult males and females can be distinguished in the field. Male and female adult Snowy Owls look different enough that they were originally classified as two different species in 1746 by Carl Linnaeus, the creator of the current system for assigning genus and species names to organisms.

The oldest adult males are almost entirely white with sparse black or brown flecks or spots. Females of a similar age appear darker with more dark bars. Caution is warranted when attempting to identify them, though, as some younger adult males may come close to being as dark as some of the palest adult females. Adult females are, as with most owls, larger than males, but the difference is quite pronounced in Snowy Owls. Being larger helps females better survive times when lemming populations are low and also improves their ability to keep the eggs and young warm.

TOP: *The warm golden glow of the rising sun signals the last hunt of the day for this Snowy Owl hovering against the winter wind along the Pacific.*

BOTTOM: *The cool purple hues of an Arctic sunset greet a Snowy Owl as it rises from the tundra for its evening hunt. During times and places where the sun sets, Snowy Owls hunt primarily between sunrise and sunset.*

Positively confirming the sex of juveniles is much more difficult than widely believed. Snowy Owls are covered with white feathers when they hatch. By the time they leave the nest they are charcoal gray but gradually lose much of their dark markings with age. It takes several years for the owls to attain their full adult plumage; the darkness and number of markings on females can continue to change as they age, though they always retain at least some dark bars. This means that juvenile males who have not yet lost their markings, may resemble adult females.

Perhaps the easiest way to positively establish the sex of a Snowy Owl in the field is to see the owl engaged in gender-specific behavior, such as the female brooding nestlings on the tundra or the male in courtship display. To see the male feeding the brooding female on the nest is the most obvious of all.

RIGHT: *Tombstones make great perches on the Arctic tundra, a place with few options high enough off the ground for effective hunting.*

OPPOSITE: *The tiny ear-tufts of the Snowy Owl are rarely visible except when the owl is flying against a strong wind, when a female is on the nest, or when interacting aggressively with another Snowy Owl.*

In addition to utilizing higher perches, visual hunters like the Snowy Owl also hover to see prey from greater distances.

ABOVE: *Fluffing their feathers allows Snowy Owls and other birds to capture pockets of air between the feathers, boosting their insulation power.*

OPPOSITE: *Older adult male Snowy Owls often appear nearly pure white, but some, like this one, retain round dark flecks on their wings, tail, or even head.*

ABOVE: *The formidable spread of the Snowy Owl's razor-sharp talons enable it to subdue not only lemmings but larger prey such as hares, sea ducks, and sometimes even small Arctic foxes.*

OPPOSITE: *Tundra mounds, like the one this Snowy Owl is flying from, are common locations for Snowy Owl nests since the wind keeps them drier and largely snow-free. Plus, they offer a better vantage point from which to spot prey or predators.*

RANGE, HABITAT, & MOVEMENTS

The Snowy Owl is a circumpolar species breeding almost exclusively in small pockets within a narrow rim of Arctic tundra from Alaska through Scandinavia to Russia. Within this range most breeding is confined to Canada, the United States (Alaska), Greenland, and Russia, with periodic breeding in Norway, Sweden, and Finland and much less frequent breeding in Iceland and Scotland (Shetland Islands). No other owl species breeds or winters so far north and so far from major population centers. Because of this, Snowy Owls are most often seen by people only during the winter, when the birds migrate south into southern Canada and the northern United States and into parts of northern Europe, Russia, and Asia. In North America they migrate into the Great Plains of southern Canada and the northern United States, to the Intermountain West, along the Great Lakes, into the St. Lawrence Valley, and along the Northeast and, less frequently, the Northwest coasts. That said, during exceptional "irruption" winters (when the owls appear in unusually large numbers both inside and outside their normal range), they may show up in places where they aren't typically seen, such as almost anywhere in the United States and Canada.

The Snowy Owl is usually categorized as a diurnal owl, meaning that it is active during the day, but the truth is far more complicated. Since the owls nest in places that experience months of nonstop daylight, they must hunt when the sun is out, but birds that remain in the Arctic during the winter must be active in the dark as well. Are they thus also nocturnal?

According to my observations, which have spanned all four seasons, they clearly become more active in periods of low light. In seasons when the sun sets, they become active at dusk and begin roosting just after sunrise. That said, they

Most Snowy Owls, such as this first-year juvenile, migrate during the winter. It can be difficult to determine the sex or age of all but the oldest adults, but one clue is that irregular, dark blotches on the face are rarely found on any but the youngest juveniles.

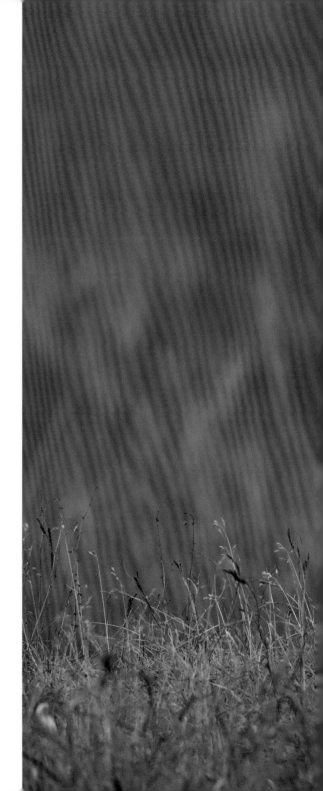

RIGHT: *As the tundra colors turn from yellows to reds, snow is imminent, and many Snowy Owls, such as this first-year juvenile, begin to migrate.*

PREVIOUS SPREAD: *During most winters, one would be lucky to encounter one Snowy Owl near the cities on the West and East Coasts, but during irruption years large numbers are sometimes seen. This particular group of five was roosting along Puget Sound, just a few hours away from both Seattle, Washington, and Vancouver, British Columbia.*

are often more active during the day if nighttime weather makes capturing their target prey more difficult, such as when freezing nighttime temperatures on barren ground make rodents less active on the surface. My observations match those of researchers across the United States and Canada who have found that the vast majority of Snowy Owl activity occurs between the early evening and the early morning, although weather, prey availability, and other factors can impact this behavior. Even during the Arctic summer, when the sun never sets, they continue to prefer the hours when one might expect darkness. When Snowy Owls are not hunting, they typically roost on the ground or, where available, on the tops of buildings.

Snowy Owls are, for the most part, territorial. The size of an individual owl's territory is based primarily upon prey populations, and when prey is abundant, owls tolerate smaller territories. During the winter some owls, particularly irrupting young owls, may roost near one another, but older owls show much less tolerance and often will drive off competitors and defend a hunting territory, particularly when food is more scarce.

Habitat

From a distance the Arctic can look flat in many places, but its ubiquitous contours are critical to the Snowy Owl's survival. The owls nest on tundra locations that feature prominent raised sites, which also are useful for roosting and hunting. These sites may be ridges, hummocks, or tundra mounds with commanding views over the surrounding landscape that are exposed to more wind and sun, thus experiencing earlier snowmelt. The owls' favored locations are frequently close to water, often the sea, and are surrounded by productive lemming habitat. Adult owls use the tundra's many ridges to shelter from the wind or hide from predators, and the young hide in divots and crevices.

During the winter Snowy Owls prefer places that are structurally similar to their nesting habitat—open areas with long lines of sight all around, which

After taking flight from a tundra mound, a Snowy Owl scans the surrounding landscape for prey.

Snowy Owls' winter habitat usually resembles their breeding habitat in that it is treeless, open, and relatively flat.

ABOVE: *The end of a sled serves as an adequate perch for hunting lemmings on the Arctic tundra.*

OPPOSITE: *Snowy Owls are normally quite territorial, but sometimes during irruptions individuals, particularly juveniles like these, can be exceptionally tolerant of one another.*

facilitates spotting prey and predators. They show a strong preference for treeless or even shrubless locations but will tolerate some of each when they have large open areas to hunt and a good food supply. Some typical winter locations include coastlines, prairies, large beaches, farm fields, marshes, pack ice on open water, cities and towns adjacent to open areas, forest openings, and often, unfortunately for the owls, airports.

Migrations, Irruptions, and Other Movements

Snowy Owls exhibit a wide and complex range of movement patterns. Some migrate, some irrupt, some travel hundreds of miles in search of food, and some stay put on breeding territories. The type of movement is influenced by a number of factors: the prior year's breeding success, snow depth, weather, and the abundance of lemmings and secondary prey such as Willow Ptarmigan, hares, and seabirds during the breeding season. It is also affected by the availability in winter of all those foods plus other birds and small mammals. The owls' unpredictable movements combined with the fact that their breeding grounds are so inaccessible make it difficult for us to estimate their actual population numbers and their exact movement patterns.

Every year between late October and early January most migratory North American Snowy Owls fly south from their breeding grounds to wintering areas in southern Canada and the northern United States. Some travel west into Russia, while others move north onto the frozen Arctic Ocean, where they feed on seabirds that congregate along openings in the ice. Snowy Owls sometimes winter thousands of miles from where they spent the previous winter.

During Snowy Owl irruptions, large numbers of owls may congregate, resulting in confrontations such as this one.

The largest Snowy Owl migrations happen during irruption years, which occur periodically in eastern and central North America but much less frequently in the west. Irruptions involve mostly young Snowy Owls that show up in unusually large numbers and often in uncommon places outside of regular wintering grounds. Until recently, it was widely believed that these irruptions were the result of a cyclical decline in lemmings, which resulted in starving owls migrating south in search of food. This caused people to think that the irruptions could be predicted and that the visiting owls were starving. However, while low prey levels may play a small role in the southward movement of owls in some years, large irruptions are more likely related to prey abundance and breeding success during the most recent breeding season with the unusually large number of young-of-year owls moving south for the winter. And while lemming populations reportedly follow rough cyclical patterns in some parts of the Arctic, they do not in others making it difficult to accurately predict irruptions.

Irruptions frequently are a regional phenomenon, but sometimes they are broader. Two relatively recent significant North American irruptions occurred during the winters of 2011–2012, when Snowy Owls showed up in thirty-five states and in all ten Canadian provinces, and in 2013–2014, when they appeared in the more typical regional pattern but in huge numbers from New England to the Great Lakes. During major irruptions owls can sometimes show up as far away from their typical wintering grounds as Utah, Texas, Oklahoma, Arkansas, South Carolina, Florida, and Bermuda! Some major irruptions are followed by smaller "echo" irruptions the following year, with owls appearing in some of the areas they visited in the prior year, but in smaller numbers.

Snowy Owls typically begin migrating back to breeding areas between February and April, with adult owls generally leaving their wintering grounds at the beginning of this period. Since Snowy Owls may not successfully breed until their fourth year, during major irruptions some juveniles remain on wintering grounds into May. After these irruptions, a very small number of juveniles may stay into, and sometimes through, the summer.

During irruptions, when Snowy Owls concentrate in large numbers, a wide variety of markings can be seen—from nearly pure white to almost completely covered with black bars. However, it is difficult and often impossible to positively establish sex in the field or through photos.

A Snowy Owl confronts a raven that is attempting to drive it away. Ravens and many other birds instinctively react with aggression to owls of all species because many species feed upon both adult birds and their nestlings.

Three irrupting Snowy Owls tolerate one another on the shores of Puget Sound and in the shadows of the Cascades. During irruptions, Snowy Owls may winter in unusual places such as near large cities like Seattle.

Most owls are inactive during windy weather, but Snowy Owls will sometimes use moderate wind to their advantage, flying into the incoming wind and using it to help them hover as they search for prey.

Snowy Owls often initiate flight with deep, strong strokes of their wings while their feet dangle, to be lifted against the torso only once the takeoff is complete.

BREEDING

Snowy Owl breeding is just as enigmatic as their migrations, but one thing is clear: the degree of success or failure is driven by the male's ability to successfully hunt a large number of lemmings. Without them, the male will not attract a mate, convince her to breed, or enable her to lay eggs. Once a male owl has secured a mate and she has scraped a nest into the top of a tundra mound, the female begins to lay eggs, and the male feeds her at the nest while she incubates the eggs and cares for the nestlings.

A spike in lemmings had driven a successful breeding season the first time I photographed Snowy Owls one July on Alaska's North Slope along the Arctic Ocean. I visited several nest sites with researchers from the Owl Research Institute. After running, crouching, and ducking to avoid attacks from a vigilant male during our survey, we counted the prey, eggs, and young and weighed the nestlings.

Plump dead lemmings outnumbered eggs at the first nest we visited. Ten lemmings were scattered around the edges of the shallow depression scraped into the sod of the tundra, with three pure white eggs bunched together in the center. This was a hopeful sign. The male seemed able to secure enough lemmings to feed his mate and the forthcoming young.

Lemming numbers spike and plummet in what has been called a cyclical—but would be more accurately called an unpredictable—fashion, with gains and declines happening both between and within nesting seasons. In early spring, when the plump rodents are still living and foraging beneath the snow-covered tundra, Snowy Owls begin concentrating where lemmings are most abundant.

Male Snowy Owls are driven to catch and stockpile as many lemmings as they can, to provide their own food for courtship and to enable the female to lay eggs. Prior to securing a mate, the male frequently stockpiles lemmings near habitual perches, which are often the most elevated parts of the tundra.

A female Snowy Owl looks over her young on their nest on the Arctic tundra. Females lay eggs roughly every two days and produce up to eight to twelve eggs if food is plentiful, resulting in young of varying ages at a single nest.

Snow can fall well into a Snowy Owl's nesting season, challenging nesting females at the very time they must stay at the nest to brood eggs and young. However, the female's coloration camouflages her particularly well during this time when the ground is a mix of white, gold, and black.

RIGHT, TOP: *As a female owl quickly leaves the nest to receive prey from her mate, her feet lift the wing of one of the nestlings.*

RIGHT, BOTTOM: *Three lemmings cached in the nest by a male Snowy Owl sit alongside the female's eggs.*

OPPOSITE, TOP: *A female Snowy Owl feeds one of her nestlings while keeping the other three beneath and one beside her warm.*

OPPOSITE, BOTTOM: *An older nestling stretches its neck to receive prey from its mother while a younger nestling stays beneath her to keep warm.*

Courtship and Mating

Snowy Owl courtship and mating take place between late April and early June, and the young, when produced, are in the nests between early June and late July. Because of their nomadic behavior, Snowy Owls are not believed to have a strong pair bond from year to year but are mostly monogamous within a breeding season. The owls, particularly the females, are not known to have much fidelity to a site or even a region. A Snowy Owl might breed in Russia, northern Canada, or Alaska in consecutive years or may skip breeding for one or several years altogether if conditions are not right. Studies have shown that it is not unusual for Snowy Owls to nest hundreds of miles from the previous year's nest site and from their natal nest. Across the narrow strip of the world's circumpolar tundra habitat Snowy Owls have nested in many places that remain vacant most years.

Given the unpredictability of these birds' migration and breeding, it took me years of trying before I finally arrived at the right place and time to witness their courtship, as described in the opening pages of this book. It was hard not to feel anxious for the male, who was constantly alert—to prey, potential mates, and potential rivals.

It also became immediately clear why each sex wears its particular pattern of feathers. When the male arrives on the tundra or begins courtship, he can easily hide by roosting on the snowy tundra or make himself visible to mates or rivals by perching on a snow-free patch or displaying against a dull sky. The female, on the other hand, is at her most vulnerable when she is on a windswept tundra mound, so her mottled pattern evolved to blend into the mosaic of turf and snow when she is in the nest. The male may retreat to a snow-covered bank, but the female must stay put until their young are old enough to keep themselves warm.

Each of my journeys to the Arctic begins with a great deal of apprehension, which often persists throughout much of the trip, since there is no way of knowing when or if the owls will arrive and if they will find enough lemmings to successfully court and breed. Even when things start out with promise, they can end with

A male Snowy Owl, lemming in bill, raises his wings and turns in circles, waving the prey as he calls.

A male Snowy Owl attempts to deliver a Lapland Longspur to his young at the nest. Normally the male delivers prey to the female who in turn feeds the young. In this situation, the female eventually interceded, snatching the prey from her mate and feeding the young herself.

disappointment if the lemmings, and thus the owls, disappear. My chances of witnessing courtship are always very small.

The temperature of negative 10 degrees Fahrenheit felt even colder that April morning on the tundra as an icy wind blew in from the nearby Arctic Ocean. I stood at my tripod, hidden behind a snowdrift in my snowy camouflage, trying to limit how often I pressed my bare finger against the metal of my camera while also trying to keep my chattering teeth from causing it to vibrate. My heart lifted each time the male successfully plucked a lemming from the shallow snow and deposited it atop the one snow-free hill on the landscape. I fretted when groups of cackling Glaucous Gulls and a cagey Arctic fox stole the entire stockpile. The thieves were confronted and driven off, but the damage was done. The male pressed on, continuing to stockpile lemmings at the location he used to initiate his courtship displays whenever a female appeared.

The male's ritualistic display with lemming in bill is a prerequisite for successful mating. I had earlier witnessed a male driven off with bites and screams as he was trying to mount a female without performing the courtship displays, and I had seen a male ignored while he waved what appeared to be a frozen piece of turf while doing the proper display.

Before beginning his courtship displays, the male must advertise his presence to prevent any nearby females from passing him by and to ward off competitors. His most far-reaching tool is a booming call that may carry up to two miles. To make this call, and perhaps for visual effect as well, the male continues the ritual by filling his throat with air and, with each hoot, bowing his head, lifting his tail, and leaning forward, his whole body seeming to vibrate with the effort. Periodically, he lifts his wings at the shoulder and spreads his tail, creating a broad, white reflective surface, and moves in circles with a lemming dangling from his bill, occasionally lifting it and waving it side to side. Watching this spectacle unfold at the highest point of land, with the Arctic Ocean to one side and the tundra to the other, made me think of an angel at the edge of the earth.

From atop a tundra ridge, his throat filled with air, wings held low, tail raised, and body lunging forward, a male Snowy Owl pushes his courtship calls through his closed bill.

LEFT: *A female Snowy Owl atop her nest watches as a Pomarine Jaeger flies low overhead.*
RIGHT: *Raising her wings and screaming a warning, a female Snowy Owl prepares to leap talons-first toward an attacking Pomarine Jaeger.*

A Pomarine Jaeger attacks a Snowy Owl as she returns to her nest to look after her young.

Often the display ends with a pause before the male, lemming still in his bill, takes flight with exaggerated wingbeats followed by extended pauses, creating a theatrical, bouncy path across the sky. It is easy to see how the slow, undulating flight itself might arrest the attention of any females, but it also allows the male to use his reflective white feathers to improve his chances.

The flight frequently ends with the male holding his erect wings up and dropping gradually downward, landing atop a prominent mound, presumably a potential nesting location. After a pause, the male often resumes calling and displaying, and if no females respond, he may either perch on the mound, looking for other owls or prey, or he may take flight.

When a female appears on the tundra nearby, the male continues the ground display for much longer. If the female flies closer, the male's display becomes more focused, though he keeps his back toward her. Occasionally the male turns toward the female, lemming in bill, while continuing his display. Eventually the female approaches the male, and the male offers her the lemming as they face each other, bill to bill. The two owls touch each other with the stiff feathers around their bills, close their eyes, and emit a soft chitter much like the one made by nestlings as they receive prey from the female. Sometimes after accepting the prey, the female will take her copulation posture, with her tail raised and her back to the male. The male mounts the female with his wings spread and tail down so that their cloacas touch for several seconds, after which the male jumps off and both vocalize. If the female produces eggs, the male continues to provision her while she remains with their eggs and potentially their young for the next several weeks until the young leave the nest.

Nesting

The Snowy Owl is one of the only owls that creates its own nests, which are located on elevated, windswept ground. The several nesting sites that I have visited were all tundra mounds between three and nine feet above the surrounding landscape, but

A male Snowy Owl, lemming in bill, displays for a female from atop a windswept tundra mound in early spring. Should the female accept his offering they will likely attempt to nest together.

in other areas, the sites may be on a variety of windswept places, free of snow early in the season, such as the crest of a hill or an elevated piece of turf.

In all cases, the owls select exposed areas that are the driest and earliest snow-free places, which provide them with the ability to see predators long before they arrive, and gives them time to slip unseen and fly low off the backside of a mound. The female likely chooses a nest site atop one of these raised locations within a male's territory, scratching a circular bowl, called a scrape, to serve as a nest. She sometimes creates a second scrape on the lee side of the mound, where she can safely move the young out of strong winds and bad weather. Normally, nothing is added to these scrapes, although sometimes feathers accumulate.

Breeding consumes prodigious amounts of energy for all birds, but even more so when an owl is breeding in such a severe habitat, as the Snowy Owl does, with unpredictable weather and food supplies. In order to survive and produce young, the female must be healthy with ample fat reserves. There will be times when food is in shorter supply. Perhaps as a hedge, the female will not lay any eggs at all without an abundance of lemmings. The female Snowy Owl typically lays anywhere from four to eight eggs, with roughly two days but sometimes as many as four days between each. Exceptionally, clutch sizes of up to fourteen have been reported.

The female begins incubating the eggs immediately after the first is laid. During this period she lies in the nest with her head low and her belly and breast against the eggs. To facilitate keeping the eggs warm, the female develops a brood patch—an area of her underside where feathers fall out to expose a bare patch of skin with a high concentration of blood vessels close to the surface—to transfer heat to the eggs when they are incubating.

Nestlings and Fledglings

Nestlings, which have a thin layer of wet, white feathers, emerge from the eggs after approximately thirty-two days. By the end of their first day, the nestlings wear fluffy, white down that will gradually turn charcoal gray.

A male Snowy Owl delivers a lemming to his mate atop their nest mound as the young run toward their next meal.

A few days after walking off of their nest mound, two juveniles huddle together in the cotton grass.

From the time she lays her first eggs until most or all of the young have left, the female leaves the nest only to defecate, receive food from the male, and occasionally redirect a predator. She normally tears prey up for smaller nestlings, but by about two weeks old they are usually able to swallow their prey whole. As a rule, the male does not begin feeding the young until they leave the nest, although I have witnessed ill-fated attempts. I once watched, amused, as a male swung a lemming in front of his youngsters while they watched without grabbing for it as they would from their mother. It seemed to me that he was swinging the prey so fast that the nestlings had a hard time keeping up with it and that the prey was oversized for their young mouths. The female showed up pretty quickly, and aggressively thwarted the male's attempts by ripping the prey from his bill.

At two weeks the nestlings begin to waddle in and out of the nest bowl, and by three weeks they are agile on foot and leave the mound, often on separate days and in the order that they hatched. The young hide in the nooks and crannies of the tundra, sometimes alone and sometimes alongside their siblings. The adults, particularly the females, frequently roost nearby. Once the young are outside the nest, the male begins feeding those young directly.

At about four weeks of age, young owls make their first attempts to fly, and by seven to eight weeks they are capable of sustained flight. At this time, they are beginning to hunt on their own. They then disperse far from their parents and are fully independent before migration begins in October.

ABOVE: *One by one, young owls walk or run off the nest and into the surrounding tundra vegetation. The young typically leave on different days with the oldest ones leaving first.*

OPPOSITE, TOP: *Six Snowy Owl nestlings huddle together for warmth at their nest.*

OPPOSITE, BOTTOM: *A week or so after the young owls leave the nest, the feathers of the feet, wings, and face of fledglings become increasingly white.*

HUNTING

Watching Snowy Owls hunt is a privilege usually afforded only to those who are willing to be patient, cold, and sleep deprived. I am afraid to estimate how many hours I have spent following and observing Snowy Owls from inside blinds, atop snowshoes, or on my belly covered in snow. I always begin by following an owl from a distance in order to gauge how close I can get without altering its behavior. Normally the owl allows me to get nearer by the hour, but rarely close enough for the owl's image to fill more than a quarter of my camera's viewfinder, using 840mm of glass (a 600mm lens plus a 1.4x teleconverter). During the vast majority of time when I'm observing an owl hunting from the ground or from a perch, it stares fixedly in one direction for hours before switching its gaze.

Snowy Owls are often drawn to the highest perches, where they can take advantage of their keen eyesight to spot prey far across the treeless expanse of the tundra. I had often wondered how they managed to find spiking lemming populations so quickly when the highest tundra mounds are, at most, several feet high. A juvenile Snowy Owl unlocked part of that secret for me one fall day on the Alaskan tundra.

I followed the owl almost eleven miles on foot across the tundra, with the Arctic Ocean at my back, from the 8:43 a.m. sunrise to sunset at 7:50 p.m. As I photographed this owl with a 600mm lens and a 2x teleconverter, I gradually moved closer, making sure the owl would still be able to hunt successfully. Although many Snowy Owls are quite skittish, this individual was capturing lemmings within thirty feet of me! In fact, at one point it was securing lemmings on almost 30 percent of its dives. As I expected it would, the owl moved across the landscape, landing at each successive large mound, where it spent anywhere from several minutes to a few hours scanning its surroundings before taking flight toward either prey or another mound.

A juvenile Snowy Owl flies from a cliff alongside the Arctic Ocean.

Unexpectedly, the wind began to rip across the tundra at fifteen to twenty miles an hour. Most birders and photographers know that it is fruitless to look for owls on windy and rainy days, so I was ready for a lull in activity. Instead, the owl found an exponentially higher perch—the wind. It continued hunting at a similar rate, although instead of waiting until it found prey before taking flight, it would fly directly into the wind and hover about twenty to thirty feet above the ground for up to several minutes at a time, rotating its head, before either diving toward a lemming or flying several dozen yards ahead to hover again, always facing the wind. I ran across the irregular, pond-pocked face of the tundra, trying not to trip, while staying ahead of, but still at a good distance from, the owl.

Suddenly, the owl flew in my direction and hovered above a snow fence, where I noticed a flock of fifteen to twenty Willow Ptarmigan roosting out of the wind. I expected the owl to dive toward a lemming, but instead it hovered lower until the skittish birds took flight and scattered across the tundra. The young owl gave chase to a particular ptarmigan before being distracted by two Arctic foxes attempting to capture the same bird. The owl stopped its pursuit and stood its ground against the approaching canines as the bird disappeared into the folds of the tundra. Although the juvenile didn't succeed in catching its prey, I was thrilled to have witnessed both its hunting of ptarmigan and the way it used the wind to aid its efforts.

Diversity of Prey

The survival of Snowy Owls depends upon a plentiful supply of lemmings during the nesting season, even though they hunt a wide variety of animals the rest of the year. Snowy Owls may eat up to a pound of food a day, and lemmings provide by far the most calories for the least effort. During the nesting season they may represent more than 90 percent of a Snowy Owl's diet. A bountiful supply of lemmings, including both the brown and collared species in North America, plays a major role in how many owls nest and how many young survive. That said, even during their breeding season, Snowy Owls supplement lemmings opportunistically with a wide

After capturing a lemming, a Snowy Owl takes flight.

variety of prey, including but not limited to hares, voles, ptarmigan, passerines as small as Snow Buntings, and seabirds as large as eiders.

Snowy Owls eat a wider variety of food during the winter, not only because lemmings are hidden beneath the snow then, but also because many owls migrate to places without lemmings at the very time they must consume more calories. In fact, various studies have indicated that a wintering Snowy Owl may consume 10 to 25 percent of its own body weight per day. Its winter diet can be quite varied, although it is primarily composed of rodents and birds. Snowy Owls have been shown to eat mice, rats, rabbits, skunks, ducks, geese, shorebirds, kestrels, harriers, other owls (Barn and Short-eared), passerines, and even fish, herons, and carrion. A friend of mine witnessed a Snowy Owl lifting an Arctic fox by the head and killing it, and I, too, have seen one eating an Arctic fox; however I am not sure if the fox was alive or dead when the owl encountered it.

Although this diversity of prey is impressive, the owls seem to specialize in prey that provides the most caloric reward per effort where they winter, and a few types of prey, or even one type, may predominate. Along the coasts it is often seabirds, and on the plains, voles; in cities, rats and pigeons are their most common prey.

Built for Hunting

A predator's physical features often hint at how it hunts and what prey it can handle. Owls have several special features that work together to aid them in finding and catching their prey, including low wing loading (weight per inch of wing surface), silent flight, and a distinctive facial disk. The lower the wing loading, the more buoyancy in flight, which is quite beneficial for owls that seek prey in flight. Most owls also possess fringe-like leading edges on their primary wing feathers to muffle sound that might otherwise alert prey. Finally, owls have a distinctive facial disk, a frame of stiff feathers around the face connected by muscular flaps, enabling them to change the shape of the disk to better capture faint sounds. When used in combination, all these features allow an owl to more accurately pinpoint the exact location

Water flies from the feathered feet of a Snowy Owl as it launches from the wet tundra.

of potential prey by sound while flying and hovering. An owl's feet also hint at what prey it captures, with larger, more powerful feet belonging to those owl species that take larger prey.

Although the Snowy Owl possesses each of these typical owl features, it has the highest wing loading of any owl, a less pronounced facial disk than most, and less fringing on its primaries than its nearest relative, the Great Horned Owl. The Snowy Owl's heavier body allows it to dive faster, and although it can detect prey with its hearing, it is more dependent upon its keen long-distance eyesight. Finally, its powerful feet allow it to subdue large prey, with the feathers covering its toes providing not just insulation but also protection from its prey's teeth and claws.

Snowy Owls scan the landscape from elevated perches—anything from the top of a tundra mound or a cliff to a telephone pole. Upon sighting prey, a Snowy raises its head, stiffens its posture, and bolts swiftly toward its target. Most of the time when it drops it uses its strong feet and sharp talons to kill the target. Less frequently, the owls pluck their prey from the ground and continue flying. They also may use their fast flight to overtake or even outmaneuver avian prey or to hover over potential prey, which they can do even in strong winds because of their powerful wings.

When elevated hunting and roosting sites are in short supply, Snowy Owls utilize any available option, including in this case the wooden shell of a skin boat.

OPPOSITE, TOP: *A heavy body and relatively silent wings allow a Snowy Owl to swiftly fly, talons open, toward an unsuspecting lemming.*

OPPOSITE, BOTTOM: *After grabbing its prey, the owl pushes its wings forward and lifts its tail to stop its momentum.*

RIGHT, TOP: *The Snowy Owl flies with the lemming in order to consume it away from other owls, as well as jaegers, foxes, ravens, and gulls.*

RIGHT, BOTTOM: *The Snowy Owl consumes the lemming after bringing it to a more defensible location.*

ABOVE: *After an ill-fated attempt to pluck a shorebird from a flock, a Snowy Owl takes flight in front of the incoming surf along the Pacific Ocean.*

OPPOSITE: *A Snowy Owl leans forward with wings raised in preparation for gliding toward unsuspecting prey.*

THE FUTURE

The shrinking of the Snowy Owl's limited breeding habitat presents major challenges to its survival. At the same time, both its breeding and wintering habitats are threatened by climate change and resource extraction. To save this species, we must understand the threats facing these owls and what we can do to help.

Threats to the Snowy Owl

Most of the world's specialized species are losing habitat due to climate change, but Arctic species such as the Snowy Owl and the lemmings they rely on as food are unique in that their breeding habitat is being pinched off, or more accurately, "melted off," on both its northern and southern edges. At the same time, significant parts of the owl's breeding and wintering habitats are being threatened by resource extraction, and its wintering habitat faces additional pressure from conversion to agriculture. The Snowy Owl's future becomes more worrisome when we add the additional impacts of development that occur around resource extraction, the use of poisons for "pest" control, and human encounters.

Climate change is already dramatically affecting the Arctic, shrinking the owl's limited suitable nesting habitat. Snowy Owls nest on the very thin band of Arctic tundra, a herbaceous habitat located between the boreal forest and the Arctic Ocean and consisting of an intricate weave of the green, yellow, red, and white fibers of mosses, lichens, sedges, grasses, wildflowers, liverworts, and some low shrubs. Only plants with short roots can survive on the thin layer of soil that rests on a frozen layer of subsoil, the permafrost. Very little precipitation falls on Arctic tundra, and most of what does fall is snow. Permafrost prevents water from soaking deeper into the ground, resulting in the presence of innumerable openings

Snow-encrusted grass is one sign of the end of the Arctic fall and the commencement of winter migration.

Female Snowy Owls rarely leave their young alone and quickly return when they do. Here, a female walks toward her waiting nestlings after flying to the nest mound.

Lemming populations are erratic, skyrocketing and plummeting from year to year and even within the same year. When populations are high, Snowy Owls may have many young, but when they are low, young will sometimes starve. In the face of a lemming shortage a female is forced to feed her starved nestling to its sibling.

RIGHT: *A gas pipeline sign serves as a perch for hunting and feasting on a lemming. While the signpost is convenient for the owl, resource extraction disturbs the permafrost and alters the fragile tundra ecosystem.*

OPPOSITE: *A polar bear stands atop the jawbone of a bowhead whale. Polar bears and Snowy Owls are both inextricably linked to and dependent upon an Arctic ecosystem that is being altered by climate change sooner and more severely than anywhere else on Earth.*

WARNING
GAS PIPELINE

of fresh water that serve the needs of millions of nesting and migrating birds. Caribou, musk oxen, Willow Ptarmigan, and most importantly, the naturally fluctuating populations of brown lemmings and collared lemmings, feed on the vegetation uniquely adapted to this tundra ecosystem. In turn, Snowy Owls, Short-eared Owls, and Arctic foxes have population cycles dependent on the lemmings. Polar bears, wolves, and wolverines feed on a wide range of other animals, many of which also feed on lemmings and require the tundra for denning.

Climate change threatens the Arctic tundra ecosystem by shrinking the area covered by permafrost, causing a loss of standing water and allowing deeper-rooting plants such as woody shrubs and trees to grow farther north, eliminating lemming habitat. Less snowfall means lemmings may also lose the insulating layer of snow that allows them to survive and multiply during the Arctic winter.

Long-term declines in lemming populations would threaten the survival of the Snowy Owl, which breeds only on the Arctic tundra and relies on lemmings to drive productive breeding years. Changes in humidity and winter temperatures in Norway and Greenland have already caused lemming populations to collapse. Given the interrelationship of Snowy Owls, lemmings, and other species dependent on lemming populations, the Snowy Owl is a good barometer—or indicator species—for the health of the tundra ecosystem.

Climate change is also melting Arctic ice and thereby shrinking Snowy Owl habitat from the north. As sea ice melts, it eliminates a winter habitat for Snowy Owls that migrate north to hunt seabirds. When the sea is frozen, seabirds congregate at openings in the ice and serve as sustenance for the owls. Without the ice, Snowy Owls would no longer be able to hunt at sea.

Resource extraction is another factor impacting Arctic habitat and is either in progress or being proposed in various parts of the region, including some prime Snowy Owl nesting habitat in and around the National Petroleum Reserve on Alaska's North Slope, the largest single unit of public land in the United States. The development associated with resource extraction can destroy nest sites and alter permafrost.

The cover of a traditional Iñupiaq ice cellar serves as a hunting perch for a Snowy Owl on the tundra cliffs above the Arctic Ocean.

Encounters with humans pose additional threats to Snowy Owls. Human-caused fatalities include collisions with automobiles and conflicts at airports. It is quite common for Snowy Owls to be attracted to the open expanses and long sightlines provided by airports. Snowy Owls occasionally collide with planes and are thus sometimes killed as a precautionary measure, although fortunately some airports are attempting to trap and relocate the birds instead.

Anticoagulant rodenticides such as those that contain warfarin are becoming an increasing problem for Snowy Owls on wintering grounds. These "pest" control agents kill rodents slowly, increasing the likelihood that owls and other raptors will ingest the poisons in their prey and die as a result.

Fortunately, the subsistence hunting of Snowy Owls and their eggs is declining, although the owls have been caught in leg traps meant for Arctic foxes. Neither issue is likely to have any significant impact on Snowy Owl populations.

When Snowy Owls irrupt into the northern United States, they are attracted to open places, including public seashores, beaches, dunes, Bureau of Land Management and national forest sagelands and grasslands, as well as other public lands. Politicians and special-interest groups, particularly in the western states, including Alaska, are investing significant legislative efforts and large amounts of money to shift the control of these lands to state, local, or private entities for resource extraction, conversion to agriculture, and other for-profit activities. Challenges to the Endangered Species Act, as well as to standards for clean water and clean air, are meant to reduce the effectiveness of efforts to fight these and other attempts to use our public lands for private and corporate profit at the expense of wildlife and habitat.

A flyover by some Bald Eagles elicits a "cryptic posture" from a Snowy Owl as it attempts to disguise its owl shape by hiding its eyes and bill with the surrounding feathers and lowering its posture to closer to parallel to the ground.

These lands, also used by Short-eared Owls, Rough-legged Hawks, Peregrine Falcons, Gyrfalcons, and other raptors, plus a range of other open-country animals, may not host Snowy Owls for years until one winter they suddenly host dozens. If taken from the public and developed for private uses, these lands would likely no longer serve as wintering habitats that allow migrating owls to survive and then return north to breed on the tundra.

Finally, the Snowy Owl's appeal sometimes works against its own best interests. Far too often, birders, photographers and other curious people get too close to wintering Snowy Owls, inadvertently forcing them to expend valuable calories taking flight to new perches or roosts. We need to remember that this is normally a skittish species and learn to read its behavior to avoid stressing them. If an owl opens its eyes, changes its posture or turns as you approach, you are too close and should retreat. Most Snowy Owls are active when the light is low, and flying in the middle of the day often means they have been flushed from a perch.

Taking Action

We can only guess how many Snowy Owls remain today. Respected estimates have put worldwide numbers as low as thirty thousand and as high as two hundred thousand. When you consider that Snowy Owls are highly nomadic, show very little site fidelity, rely on a vulnerable food supply, breed relatively infrequently with fluctuating productivity in relatively small pockets of their prime habitat, you get a sense of the challenge in calculating their numbers. While a precise population number can't be confirmed, researchers agree that half of the world's Snowy Owls live in the Canadian Arctic.

In light of new research, the International Union for Conservation of Nature changed the Snowy Owl's status to "vulnerable" on its Red List of Threatened Species in December 2017.

Snowy Owls need our immediate attention and support in order to survive. The beauty and charisma of this species fascinate us; however, these owls live out much of their lives in some of the more inaccessible places on Earth and real-life encounters are rare for most people. This makes the Snowy Owl seem almost mythical and independent from our world and actions.

During irruptions when Snowy Owls arrive close to cities and small towns, they require habitat on both public and private lands, reminding us of their presence and need for protection. But their reliance upon these lands is often forgotten

We do not think of the Snowy Owl as a marine animal, but much of its life plays out alongside oceans and large lakes.

During the winter, Snowy Owls normally set up territories centered around abundant food, but sometimes during irruptions large numbers may congregate. During these times they allow others to roost near them although there are frequent squabbles.

RIGHT: *During the breeding season Snowy Owls are strictly territorial. The most dominant owls will command the best hunting and breeding sites and will aggressively drive away any competitors.*

OPPOSITE: *For owls that winter in southern Canada and the northern United States, sunrise normally signals the end of active hunting for Snowy Owls; they will then head toward safe roost sites to spend the day.*

A hunting cabin and skin boat near the Arctic Ocean serve as the center of a Snowy Owl's fall hunting territory just before deep snows compels it to migrate.

before the next irruption occurs. Our efforts must focus on two fronts: protecting the public lands on which the owls breed and winter and halting, or at least slowing, climate change so their breeding habitat does not disappear.

Achieving these goals requires us to stay informed and be willing to advocate politically and economically. Such work is impossible to accomplish alone. Consider joining a local or national conservation organization that can provide guidance on how our voices, votes, and investments can make the most impact. Communicate with your local, state, provincial, and national government representatives, vote for policies and candidates who fight for public lands and against climate change, and donate to organizations and invest in corporations that support these goals.

I hope that we heed the earnest call of the Snowy Owl, a call that is both an invitation to learn more about this charismatic animal and an urgent plea to protect both it and its vulnerable Arctic habitat.

RIGHT: *The rising moon awakens a wintering Snowy Owl. We must remember that although Snowy Owls can be active at any time of the day, during the winter they are primarily nocturnal and disturbing them on their daytime perches can challenge their ability to survive the winter.*

OPPOSITE: *Snowy Owls are the heaviest owl in North America. Their large bodies help them stay warm in the most extreme cold.*

Field Guide to the Snowy Owl

It is rare to find two Snowy Owls together, yet alone five. Such groups of Snowy Owls are sometimes seen during extreme migration years, or irruptions.

DESCRIPTION: A large, long-winged white owl; approximately 23.5 inches long, with a wingspan of 56 to 61 inches.

SIMILAR SPECIES: Heavily barred juveniles or the darkest females might be confused with whitish-colored Arctic forms of the Great Horned Owl.

INTERESTING FACT: Snowy Owls are one of the few owl species in which adult males and females show different markings, although the differences are most striking with mature adults.

NORTH AMERICAN DISTRIBUTION AND HABITAT: Some are year-round residents of the Arctic, others migrate into the Great Plains of Canada and the United States in the winter, while still others show up in other states particularly in the Great Lakes region, Northeast, and Northwest during irruption years. Exceptionally in large irruptions, birds have appeared in locations like Hawaii and the Carolinas.

■ NORMAL WINTER AND BREEDING RANGE

NESTING: A ground-nesting owl that scrapes a bowl on elevated ground on the Arctic tundra; typically lays between one and four eggs, though higher numbers— as many as 14— have been reported.

VOCALIZATION: A loud, foghorn-like *hoo-hoo* call, usually in two parts but sometimes more.

CONSERVATION STATUS: Vulnerable in North America, and declines in Europe are of concern for the United States.

Acknowledgments

It takes a team to publish a strong book and I am grateful to have benefited from a talented group. Helen Cherullo's initial embrace of the concept, Kate Rogers' insightful collaboration at each juncture, Linda Gunnarson's attention to detail and understanding of natural history, the continuous guidance and subtle improvements implemented by Janet Kimball and, finally, the beautiful design work by Kate Basart, helped create a work I am proud to share.

After missing a ptarmigan, a Snowy Owl, with talons still outstretched, flies low across the Arctic tundra.

About the Author

PAUL BANNICK is an award-winning author and photographer who captures images to inspire wildlife education and conservation. He is the author and photographer of two best-selling bird books, *Owl: A Year in the Lives of North American Owls* (Braided River, 2016) and *The Owl and The Woodpecker: Encounters with North America's Most Iconic Birds* (Mountaineers Books, 2008). *Owl* received the gold medal in the animals category of the 2017 Independent Publisher Book Awards, and *The Owl and the Woodpecker* was a finalist for the Washington State Book Award.

Paul's photography has won awards from several prestigious contests, including those hosted by *Audubon* magazine and the International Conservation Photography Awards. His work is prominently featured in bird guides from Audubon, Peterson, and the Smithsonian, among others, and has appeared in a variety of publications including the *New York Times, Audubon, Sunset, Nature's Best Photography Magazine,* and *National Geographic* online. Additionally, his photography has been the subject of many regional and national television and radio pieces as well as several North American traveling exhibits.

An active public speaker, Paul presents multimedia owl and woodpecker programs at events throughout the United States and Canada every year. He serves as the director of major gifts for Conservation Northwest, a Seattle based nonprofit dedicated to protecting, connecting, and restoring wildlands and wildlife from the coast of Washington to the Rockies of British Columbia.

More of his work can be seen at paulbannick.com, on Facebook at Paul Bannick Photography, and on Instagram @paulbannick.

A broad range of dark bars and spots cover the bodies and wings of Snowy Owls. Although it is tempting to identify the lighter birds as males and the darker birds as females, it is almost impossible to positively establish their sex in the field from a distance or from photographs unless you witness gender-specific behavior.

A Note about the Photography

I strive to capture authentic moments of natural behavior in a manner that has the most minimal impact on the subject. This allows me to photograph nature as it *is* rather than as we *wish* it appeared. I do not bait or lure subjects, and, unless explicitly noted, all of my images feature wild, unrestrained subjects. None of the images were taken with camera traps. I do not edit out distracting branches, birds, or other elements, and remove nothing but dust from the camera's sensor. I apply only global electronic modifications such as minimal levels, contrast, noise reduction, or saturation to the entire image to match what I witnessed and do not create composite images.

The images in this book were captured with Canon and Sony cameras with 600mm f4, 24-70mm f2.8, and 100-400mm lenses. Carbon tripods and gimbal heads were used for most images.

recreation • lifestyle • conservation

MOUNTAINEERS BOOKS is a leading publisher of mountaineering literature and guides—including our flagship title, *Mountaineering: The Freedom of the Hills*—as well as adventure narratives, natural history, and general outdoor recreation. Through our two imprints, Skipstone and Braided River, we also publish titles on sustainability and conservation. We are committed to supporting the environmental and educational goals of our organization by providing expert information on human-powered adventure, sustainable practices at home and on the trail, and preservation of wilderness.

The Mountaineers, founded in 1906, is a 501(c)(3) nonprofit outdoor recreation and conservation organization whose mission is to enrich lives and communities by helping people "explore, conserve, learn about, and enjoy the lands and waters of the Pacific Northwest and beyond." One of the largest such organizations in the United States, it sponsors classes and year-round outdoor activities throughout the Pacific Northwest, including climbing, hiking, backcountry skiing, snowshoeing, camping, kayaking, sailing, and more. The Mountaineers also supports its mission through its publishing division, Mountaineers Books, and promotes environmental education and citizen engagement. For more information, visit The Mountaineers Program Center, 7700 Sand Point Way NE, Seattle, WA 98115-3996; phone 206-521-6001; www.mountaineers.org; or email info@mountaineers.org.

Our publications are made possible through the generosity of donors and through sales of 700 titles on outdoor recreation, sustainable lifestyle, and conservation. To donate, purchase books, or learn more, visit us online:

MOUNTAINEERS BOOKS
1001 SW Klickitat Way, Suite 201 • Seattle, WA 98134 • 800-553-4453
mbooks@mountaineersbooks.org • www.mountaineersbooks.org
An independent nonprofit publisher since 1960